IN THE SPIRIT OF
LAS VEGAS

This book is dedicated to my daughter Alexandra who inspires my days
and to JCB whose creativity transformed my world.

—Jennifer Worthington

Cover: © Ellen von Unwerth / Art + Commerce

Text © Jennifer Worthington

© 2007 Assouline Publishing, Inc.
601 West 26th Street, 18th floor
New York, NY 10001, USA
Tel.: 212 989 6810 Fax: 212 647 0005
www.assouline.com

ISBN: 978 2 84323 885 7

Color separation: Luc Alexis Chasleries
Printed by SNP Leefung

All rights reserved.
No part of this publication may be reproduced,
stored in a retrieval system, or transmitted in any form or by any
means, electronic, mechanical, photocopying, recording, or
otherwise, without prior consent from the publisher.

JENNIFER WORTHINGTON

IN THE SPIRIT OF
LAS VEGAS

ASSOULINE

CONTENTS

Introduction	11
The Desert	14
The Meadows	18
Bugsy Siegel	31
The Rat Pack	46
Glitter Gulch	59
Elvis	70
Marriage Capital	78
The Strip	85
Howard Hughes	100
The Showgirl	107
Hotels	117
Entertainment	129
Guides	143
Copyrights & Acknowledgments	157

Introduction

Six years ago, when I told people I was moving to Las Vegas, my announcement was met with utter disbelief and jaw-dropping shock. I can't say I blamed them. I, too, was somewhat aghast that I was moving to a city most famous for its buffets and showgirls, and seemingly devoid of culture. Since then, however, I have come around. I now appreciate the uniqueness of Las Vegas, its rebellious nature and its unapologetic kitsch. And I've also learned how to truly revel in the only city in the world whose sole purpose is to provide pleasure.

To look back on the evolution of Las Vegas, which literally began as a one-horse town and is now among the fastest-growing cities in America, is an astonishing lesson in determination and survival. This is a place where the American dream can still happen, where the Gold Rush mentality is alive and well. It's also the only town where one's wildest fantasies can become a reality—usually within twenty-four hours or less!

The iconic images of the Las Vegas Strip reveal a vulgarity that is so over-the-top, so unexpected, and on such a grand scale, it becomes charming; a city where bigger really is better and gaudy is not the exception, but one of the few rules. Yet something new is happening to Las Vegas that has everyone—not just cosmopolitan transplants like myself—taking notice. Today we have the best restaurants in the world, the best entertainment, the best shopping, the best spas, and of course, the best gambling.

For locals (yes, like me) the city is a mecca where lives are changed in a refreshingly short amount of time. And where the greatest visionaries in modern history have converged to build the

A cowgirl welcomes visitors to Las Vegas.

most outrageous playground the world has ever seen.

Now when people ask me where I live and I say Las Vegas, I must admit I enjoy that initial look of shock. Every time that I fly over the Mojave Desert to this spectacular cityscape, and every morning that I wake up and see the green glow of the MGM Grand, and every day that I drive down the Las Vegas Strip, rich with history, I feel a surge of excitement and a smile spreads across my face. Watching the evolution of this one-and-only city has been a true honor, and I, once a skeptic, have been incredibly humbled. Honestly, I can't wait to see what happens next.

Jennifer Worthington
January 2007

A reveler poses in front of a neon sign.

Think of the sexiest and most stimulating painting you have ever seen, filled with vibrant color and vivid imagery. Then imagine that painting surrounded by a broad, flat, brown frame. Just a plain, dull border. It is perhaps an odd analogy for some, but for those who have made the tedious drive into the Las Vegas Valley from practically any direction, it's a reality. Las Vegas is located in the middle of the Mojave Desert, which means essentially, that it shouldn't exist in terms of climate and conditions. Little rainfall, howling winds, and one-hundred-plus degree temperatures make it virtually uninhabitable in parts. However, the city is more than a mirage, although it feels like one from a distance. The land for miles and miles around Las Vegas is forbidding. There is nothing to even hint that the jewel box of the Strip exists. Look around and you could easily be on another planet, moon rocks protruding from the ground, sandstorms dancing across the arid desert. Mountains rise up in varying height, some completely made of dirt and stone, others dotted with the brownish green of Joshua trees and cacti. Life, in any form, seems nonexistent. Spot a bighorn sheep—the Nevada state animal—and consider yourself one of the lucky few. This goes on for miles, mountain after mountain, ashy rock after ashy rock. Colors blend and fade from deep red, burnt sienna, and rosy pink, to taupe, tan, and beige. Granted, this unusual landscape has unique beauty and luster, but for those whose destination is the thrilling city of sin, the blandness of the desert becomes a record played one too many times. And just then, on the brink of perpetual nothingness, there it is. As a hill comes to a sloping crest, you see something in the distance. As you get closer, colors start to twinkle and dance, morphing from reds to yellows to blues and greens. The oasis appears out of nowhere. It is Las Vegas.

Warren Beatty and Annette Bening romance in the desert in *Bugsy* (1991).

The Meadows

Las Vegas is a land of contradiction. Where the rest of America upholds a certain lawfulness, taste, and decorum, Las Vegas runs amok, challenging the rule of order, mocking civility, distorting art and architecture, and generally, having a good time all the while.

Even its name is something of a wild discrepancy. In 1829, Rafael Rivera, a young Mexican scout, was part of larger band of Spanish traders. En route from New Mexico to California, he stumbled upon a small area of green trees, soft brush, and an abundance of natural springwater. Encouraged by this patch of life on the Spanish Trail, a notoriously difficult and dry travel route, Rivera promptly named his find "Las Vegas," which, when translated meant "The Meadows." Of course, over the next few decades, Las Vegas' first hard-scrubbed settlers would regard the arid landscape as anything but plush or rolling with green hills and spring flowers. After all, this plot of land, albeit complete with an ample water supply, was still only about 140 miles away from a barren, kiln-like landscape known the world over as Death Valley.

Before the youthful exuberance of Rivera, Paiute Indians lived off the land and were able to sustain a relatively lengthy existence, considering the harsh climate. But it was the birth of a railroad in 1904 that landed The Meadows on the map, and on the road to wanton abandon and indiscretion. Essentially a pit stop between Salt Lake City, Utah, and California, Las Vegas became a place for refueling, repairs, and rest. A Wild West town populated by a few hundred settlers, Las Vegas consisted mainly of workmen, vagabonds, and a handful of visionary entrepreneurs, lured by the prospect of land ownership. These were men working on the

Noel Coward smoking a cigarette, 1955.

Vegas' McCarran International Airport, one of the world's busiest airports.

railroad, stuck in the desert, and enticed to shell out a few hundred bucks for a plot of their own—and the promise of a fortune.

Little did they know just what kind of fortune would come about. In the midst of this burgeoning hamlet erupted a tiny strip, if you will, of vice and debauchery. Block 16 was the only part of town where people could drink, gamble, and drink some more. Needless to say, the area thrived—a harbinger, perhaps, of what was to come. Las Vegas was already subsisting on what other New West townships wouldn't abide: access to booze, cards, quickie marriages, and prostitution.

But life outside the infamous Block 16 proved more difficult. In fact, the majority of early settlers didn't stick around long enough to even give it a shot and almost immediately shuttered their businesses, scared off by the windy conditions, desolation, and shoot-'em-up mentality.

By 1930, Las Vegas was in crisis. The railroad company had changed routes, there were numerous layoffs, and travelers stopped passing through. There were no "meadows" to see here, no greenery, nothing but dust and tumbleweeds. The rest of the United States was going through its own state of emergency—the Great Depression touched almost every corner of the country.

But just as the lights were about to go out for good, Las Vegas received the first of many resuscitating visits from Lady Luck. The unlikely guardian angel came in the form of the U.S. government, strictly by way of geographic crapshoot, which offered up $175 million to build the Hoover Dam, a monstrous project to harness the Colorado River.

Soon workers landed in a government-fabricated town dubbed Boulder City, close to the dam site and about twenty-three miles from Las Vegas. This quaint 'burb was devised to be a no-gambling, no-drinking hamlet, both to snub Las Vegas and to keep the

Opposite and following pages: aerial views of the Hoover Dam.

1. A postcard of the Castaneda, one of Vegas' first hotels, 1906.
2. Las Vegas in the 1960s.
3. Gamblers playing roulette in an early casino, 1936.
4. Signs along Fremont Street, the main thoroughfare, ca. 1954.
5. Between 1909–11, the San Pedro, Los Angeles, and Salt Lake railroad constructed 64 single family dwellings for employees. These cottages were of the first tract developments in the U.S. and influenced the developments in the surrounding areas of Clarke's Las Vegas Townsite.

thousands of dam workers clean and sober and on the straight-and-narrow. Las Vegas, however, didn't mind the slight. It knew better.

Sure enough, almost immediately after the five-year project began in 1931, Las Vegas received a new jolt. Hard-working construction boys lit up the town, arriving by the truckloads on their days off, spending their paychecks in the speakeasies and now-legalized gambling halls of Block 16 and Fremont Street, where newer establishments were popping up.

By 1936, Las Vegas was well on its way to shedding the Wild West image of a dust bowl. What emerged lay the groundwork for decades to follow: years flush with money, glitz, glamour, and hundreds of thousands of visitors. The Meadows would be anything but the quiet, green oasis of calm restfulness that Rivera had imagined.

Exterior of the Moulin Rouge casino, ca. 1955.

Bugsy Siegel

In the movie, *Casino,* Robert De Niro plays a Mobbed-up Las Vegas casino executive. Sharon Stone is his gorgeous moll and Joe Pesci his violent right-hand man. It's a Hollywood film, yes, but its premise isn't that far from the early truth of Las Vegas. The Mob was a reality in Sin City, and one of the first Mafia men to make a name for himself was wiseguy Benjamin "Bugsy" Siegel.

A protégé of the legendary mob boss, Myer Lansky, Siegel was hardly the stuff of visionaries—he was a reputed mobster, a bootlegger, shyster, conman, and killer—but his idea for a hotel that allowed everything one could possibly desire sparked a trend that would last into the next millennium. Bugsy dreamed big. He wanted to rid Vegas of the tired western theme that permeated the existing hotels on the Strip and lure the classy Hollywood players, the best dames, and hottest gamblers. He ostensibly wanted to create a suped-up Monte Carlo in Nevada. In 1941 he set out to build the Flamingo. Five years later, having spent millions in Mob money to construct his vision, the luxury oasis opened its doors.

But the Flamingo didn't catch on right away. In fact, the 105-room tropical-themed hotel was essentially empty after the opening celebration went flat; bad weather, lack of finished accommodations, and no-show VIPs cemented its fate as a total dud. The hype petered out, Siegel sought refuge in Hollywood…and the Mob sought him. It was payback for the six million dollars Siegel had borrowed on a dream he couldn't deliver. In June of 1947, Bugsy was brutally murdered, shot several times in the living room of the Beverly Hills home of his girlfriend, actress Virginia Hill. Mere minutes later, back in Las Vegas, three Mafia higherups walked into the Flamingo and took over.

Gangster and playboy Benjamin "Bugsy" Siegel at the L.A. County Jail, following an indictment for a Hollywood gangland execution, 1941.

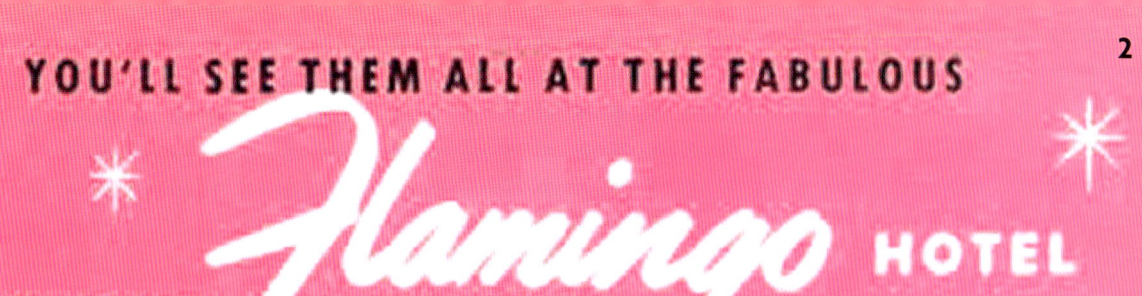

1. Bugsy Siegel and actor George Raft, 1944.
2. A postcard promoting the Flamingo Hotel.
3. Virginia Hill, Bugsy Siegel's mistress, in 1947.
4. Dealer standing at the Wheel of Fortune, 2002.
5. The Flamingo Hotel and Casino, 2005.

Following pages: A neon sign lights up a contemporary casino, 2006.

The hotel lived on, and so did the Mob. After Siegel's murder, members of the syndicate started paying attention to Vegas and soon there was a plethora of wiseguys not only shaking-down the action, but actually running the casinos. Benny Binion, a convicted criminal, arrived from Texas and the famed Horseshoe was born. Moe Dalitz, a gangster from an Ohio crime family, backed the building of the Desert Inn. In the 1970s, Frank "Lefty" Rosenthal and his right-hand Tony "the Ant" Spilotro (on whom the De Niro and Pesci characters in *Casino* were based) set up shop, skimming and strong-arming their way through the last years of Mafia reign. Before Vegas went legit, so to speak, there were Mob-connected honchos up and down the Strip and along Glitter Gulch. A builder needed cash to get his hotel running, and the Mob was there to foot the bill. The bosses back in Chicago or New York wanted to taste some of the earnings, and the small-time henchmen in Vegas would head to the back rooms to skim a little cash off the top of the take. As for law enforcement, suffice it to say, there wasn't much at the time. Or at least there weren't many who cared. The casinos were doing big business with the connected thugs running the racket. And the more money the casinos made, the bigger Vegas got, and the city reaped the rewards.

Eventually, the Mob dwindled, thanks in part to the flush of legitimate cash and real investors, from Howard Hughes to Conrad Hilton. The irony for the Mob was that their work made Vegas grow, and that growth brought more people. More people brought more regulation—putting Mob bosses out of a job. Politicians started to turn down bribes, the Gaming Control Board got clean, and entrepreneurs like Kirk Kerkorian didn't want to give the Mob a cut. After the Mafia left town, corporations took over, and they still run Vegas, for the most part. Old-timers sometimes say these giants operate the same way as the Mob once did, only they do it in suits. When the Mob left, they took their violence and brute force with them, but their departure also meant the loss of personal connection between casino executive and player. It was an era that helped put Vegas on the map for good, and brought a kind of hospitality that no other city in the world could rival. Just the way Bugsy would have wanted it.

View of gamblers taken through a one-way mirror in the ceiling of a casino.

1. Sharon Stone plays a Mob wife in *Casino* (1995).
2. Residents celebrating Helldorado, a four-day commemoration of Las Vegas history, in 1935.
3. Julia Roberts, George Clooney, Brad Pitt, and Matt Damon in the 2001 remake of *Ocean's Eleven*.
4. Sean Connery as James Bond in *Diamonds are Forever* (1971).
Following pages: Robert De Niro as Sam "Ace" Rothstein in *Casino*.

The Rat Pack

By 1960, Las Vegas was a swingin' hot spot. It was the ultimate tourist destination, with full-blown resort hotels, cash, entertainment, and more excitement than any other U.S. city, with the exception, perhaps, of New York. While the exterior of Las Vegas was becoming the epitome of kitsch, the inside of one dimly lit lounge was making it the epitome of cool. A motley crew of five musicians took the stage in the Sands hotel's Copa Room, and the world started paying attention. The Rat Pack was born.

Frank Sinatra, Dean Martin, Sammy Davis Jr., Joey Bishop, and Peter Lawford simultaneously changed the face of hip, not just in the smoky rooms they played in Las Vegas, but throughout the rest of the country. Their shows made every man, woman, boy, and girl want to mix a martini and light up a smoke.

Initially known as the Clan, they were dubbed the Rat Pack by the press after tales of the group's wild ways and impromptu bawdiness saturated popular culture. (Besides, "the Clan" wasn't exactly a friendly association.) Sinatra was the Chairman of the Board, of course, and his mood and style led the rest of the gang. Bishop, a comedian, was the de facto emcee; Martin, the drunk; Davis, the foil; and Lawford, the suave Brit.

The rise of the Rat Pack's profile quickly spawned a movie, *Ocean's Eleven*, about the robbery of five Las Vegas casinos. It was during the filming of this heist comedy caper that the Summit, as the gathering was called, came to be. The members of the Rat Pack spent their days shooting the film on the Strip and whiled away their nights doing two shows at the Copa Room to packed houses. Sleep wasn't a part of the plan as the party often continued backstage all night long.

The Rat Pack poses in front of the Sands hotel. From left to right: Frank Sinatra, Dean Martin, Sammy Davis Jr., Peter Lawford, and Joey Bishop, ca. 1960.

Bleary-eyed, they would show up on the set the next day and effortlessly do it all over again. This was the heyday of cool—the resurgence of a true boys' club where no joke, dame, or cocktail was off-limits. Their act, mostly improvised, consisted of songs, stories, and raw humor—and a rolling bar cart from which plenty of drinks were shaken and stirred.

Each time the Rat Pack took the stage, the audience never knew which members would be on board. Some nights it was just Sinatra and Martin; others, the full gang of five. During this period, Davis, Martin, and Bishop usually had their own gigs at other hotels, but there was always a good chance of a visit from other Rat Packers, and the unknowing crowds ate it up. Marquees read "DEAN MARTIN! MAYBE FRANK? MAYBE SAMMY?" and such.

The city instantly secured a unique chapter in entertainment history and morphed into a must-be locale. Seeing Sinatra and company became a coveted badge of hipness. Rat Pack fever swept through all circles—from Hollywood, where celebrities would hop the last flight to Vegas for the shows, to Washington, D.C., home of Lawford's brother-in-law John F. Kennedy. At the time, Kennedy was a handsome young senator on the presidential campaign

Bing Crosby, Frank Sinatra, Dean Martin, and Bob Hope on the set of *The Road to Hong Kong* (1962).

trail. Sinatra and Kennedy became fast friends; their relationship was the source of numerous rumors for years to come.

The Rat Pack wasn't entirely exclusive. Other stars would sometimes be invited to join in the fun, ad-libbing or roasting one member or another to the cheers of hundreds of onlookers. For her appearances, movie starlet Angie Dickinson played the role of Rat Pack Mascot. And Shirley MacLaine was given honorary Rat Packette status. Judy Garland was also a frequent surprise guest, as was Lauren Bacall.

But the electricity that the Rat Pack ignited wasn't limited to VIPs. Sinatra and his pals' signature gift for laid-back lingo and ring-a-ding-ding jive brought thousands of visitors to the Strip. Many would sleep in hotel lobbies, or even in their cars, just for the chance to nab a ticket to a sold-out Rat Pack show.

Eventually, however, the ride ran its course. By 1966 or so, the gang had all but disbanded. Each went on to pursue his showbiz dream, riding out career peaks and valleys, and often returning to the Strip for headlining gigs. Davis released more hit albums. Martin kept crooning and hosted a variety show. Bishop's shtick kept him on the comedy circuit, and Lawford, who had a falling out with Sinatra in 1962, returned to his mediocre movie career.

But Sinatra remained Las Vegas' adopted brother-in-arms. He returned to the city over the next twenty years on numerous occasions for private concerts, appearances, and celebrations, maintaining his friendships with reputed underworld characters, and occasionally reuniting with a former Rat Pack member to relive the glory days of cool. When Sinatra died in 1998, the lights were dimmed on the Las Vegas Strip in his honor.

Dean Martin pulls off the heist of a lifetime in *Ocean's Eleven* (1960).

Sammy Davis Jr. entertains at the Sands hotel.

Previous pages: A studio portrait for the film *Ocean's Eleven* (1960). Clockwise from the left: Frank Sinatra, Dean Martin, Peter Lawford, Joey Bishop, and Sammy Davis Jr.

1. Dean Martin makes his debut as a single star, ca 1957.
2. Sammy Davis Jr. a strip perennial, as seen on the back cover of *Las Vegas Magazine*.
3. Frank Sinatra as Danny Ocean with Patrice Wymore in *Ocean's Eleven*.
4. Backstage on Dean Martin's opening night at the Copa Room, March 6, 1957.

Glitter Gulch

By the mid-1950s, Las Vegas was coming into its own. Gone were the sawdust-covered floors of old poker rooms and the only-if-you-dare atmosphere of rough-and-tumble watering holes on Fremont Street. Instead, casinos polished up, laid down carpeting, put their dealers in button-down shirts, their cocktail waitresses in pantyhose and heels, and ordered custom neon signs that would become the hallmark of downtown Las Vegas. At night, the seven-block stretch of Fremont lit up so brightly that it earned the nickname Glitter Gulch.

The Young Electric Sign Company (YESCO) was the arbiter of Glitter Gulch. Purveyor of neon signs since 1925, YESCO created Las Vegas' first signature neon calling card at the Boulder Club on Fremont Street in 1945. Almost immediately, other casinos followed suit. YESCO signs were erected at the Golden Nugget, the Las Vegas Club, the Eldorado Club, and the Silver Slipper. The Mint, Hotel Fremont, Hotel Apache, and the Golden Gate also helped create the incredible nighttime spectacle.

The pièce de résistance was Vegas Vic, the forty-foot-tall friendly cowboy who tipped his neon hat and said, "Hello, partner!" to everyone who entered the old Pioneer Club. Vegas Vic became an iconic image, the undisputed inanimate mayor of Glitter Gulch. Over the years, Vic endured some hard times: faded clothes, broken lights, and the loss of his mechanical arm. But at the turn of the millennium he was refurbished and can still be found near the intersection of Las Vegas Boulevard and Fremont Street.

Truth be told, on the whole, a bit of the city's sparkle has dissipated over the past five decades. Casinos have come and gone, and the lights

Opposite and following pages: The bright lights of Glitter Gulch.

Neon signs advertising the legalized gambling establishments in downtown Las Vegas light up the night sky, 1953.

have changed. But the most serious infraction, ironically, was the growth of Las Vegas itself. The birth of the Strip and the onslaught of today's über-hotel-casinos not only drew attention away from the Gulch, but also lured hard-core gamblers and throngs of awestruck tourists. Downtown's luster faded substantially with the addition of the Mirage, the Bellagio, the Venetian, Caesars Palace, and others.

In 1998, hoping to recapture some of its signature glitz, Fremont Street unveiled a four-block-long LED light canopy. The seventeen million dollar investment cloaks a pedestrian mall and flashes a dramatic light show several times a night. With more than twelve million lightbulbs creating colors, shapes, and symbols that swirl and dance to choreographed music, it's a tourist trap, to be sure, but it's helping bring people back to Vintage Vegas.

Luckily, some of the fabulous neon signs that made up America's brightest main drag are now being refurbished and treasured, thanks in part to the efforts of the Neon Museum and Boneyard. This nonprofit organization has already restored the original Aladdin's Lamp sign, the old Hacienda's famous Horse & Rider sign, the Wedding Information sign from the 1940s, and the old Nevada Motel sign, among others. Amid all of the changes that continue to unfold at breakneck pace in Vegas, it's reassuring to know that some of the old treasures of Glitter Gulch are being saved from total extinction.

Today, past and present coexist in unique juxtaposition. Souvenir shops, street performers, and a slightly seedier element mute the twinkle of the Glitter Gulch casinos. However, downtown is in the midst of a renaissance. Led by Las Vegas mayor Oscar Goodman, a surge of redevelopment is prompting construction of urban dwellings, lofts, and a burgeoning arts district. Glitter Gulch may not exactly be what it once was, but odds are it will get lucky the second time around.

Binion's Horseshoe Hotel and Casino, home of the World Series of Poker tournament, and a Fremont Street legend since 1951.

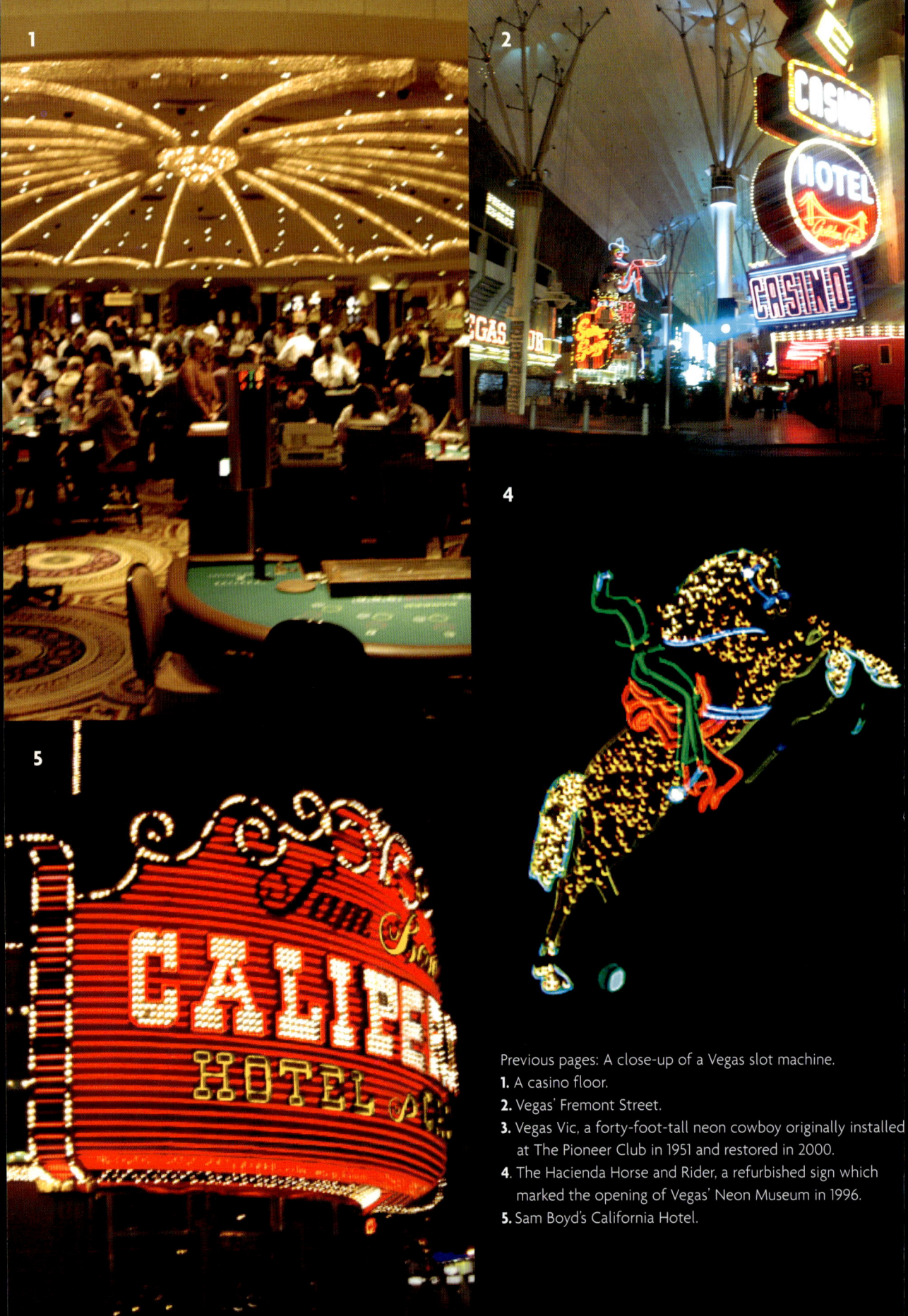

Previous pages: A close-up of a Vegas slot machine.
1. A casino floor.
2. Vegas' Fremont Street.
3. Vegas Vic, a forty-foot-tall neon cowboy originally installed at The Pioneer Club in 1951 and restored in 2000.
4. The Hacienda Horse and Rider, a refurbished sign which marked the opening of Vegas' Neon Museum in 1996.
5. Sam Boyd's California Hotel.

Elvis

In 1956, inside the lounge at the New Frontier Hotel and Casino, a young man was making a name for himself in Las Vegas. But for Elvis Presley, the attention wasn't the sort he had anticipated for his two-week stint as the opening act for comic Shecky Greene. The King bombed. It may be hard to believe, but in a town that relished bright lights, showgirls, and a pervasive faux Wild West motif, Elvis Presley was considered gauche. At the time, his wiggling hips, bluesy rock R&B, and quivering lip completely missed the mark with the adult tourists Las Vegas was hosting by the thousands. Presley, although gaining popularity with teenagers around the country, lacked a connection with audiences on the Strip in the mid-50s, still a culturally conservative time in America.

Eventually, Presley would reign, and his talents would ignite legions of fans from all walks of life. Flash forward a few years and Elvis would become the biggest thing in entertainment this century. He would return to Las Vegas in 1963, this time riding high as a singer, heartthrob, and box-office-busting movie star. With Ann-Margaret by his side, Presley immortalized the riff *Viva Las Vegas,* and today the musical movie is still considered a cult classic. He would forever be an icon.

And the town proved profitable for Presley professionally. He was a popular headliner and a regular visitor, and in 1967 he became a Vegas newlywed when he tied the knot with his longtime girlfriend, Priscilla Beaulieu, in a quickie but lavish ceremony at the old Aladdin Hotel. But by the late 1960s, Presley had plateaued. His addictions to pills and booze was getting the best of him, physically and emotionally.

In desperate need of a career boost, Presley's handlers landed him a lucrative but incredibly demanding deal at the International Hotel

Las Vegas was captivated by the King.

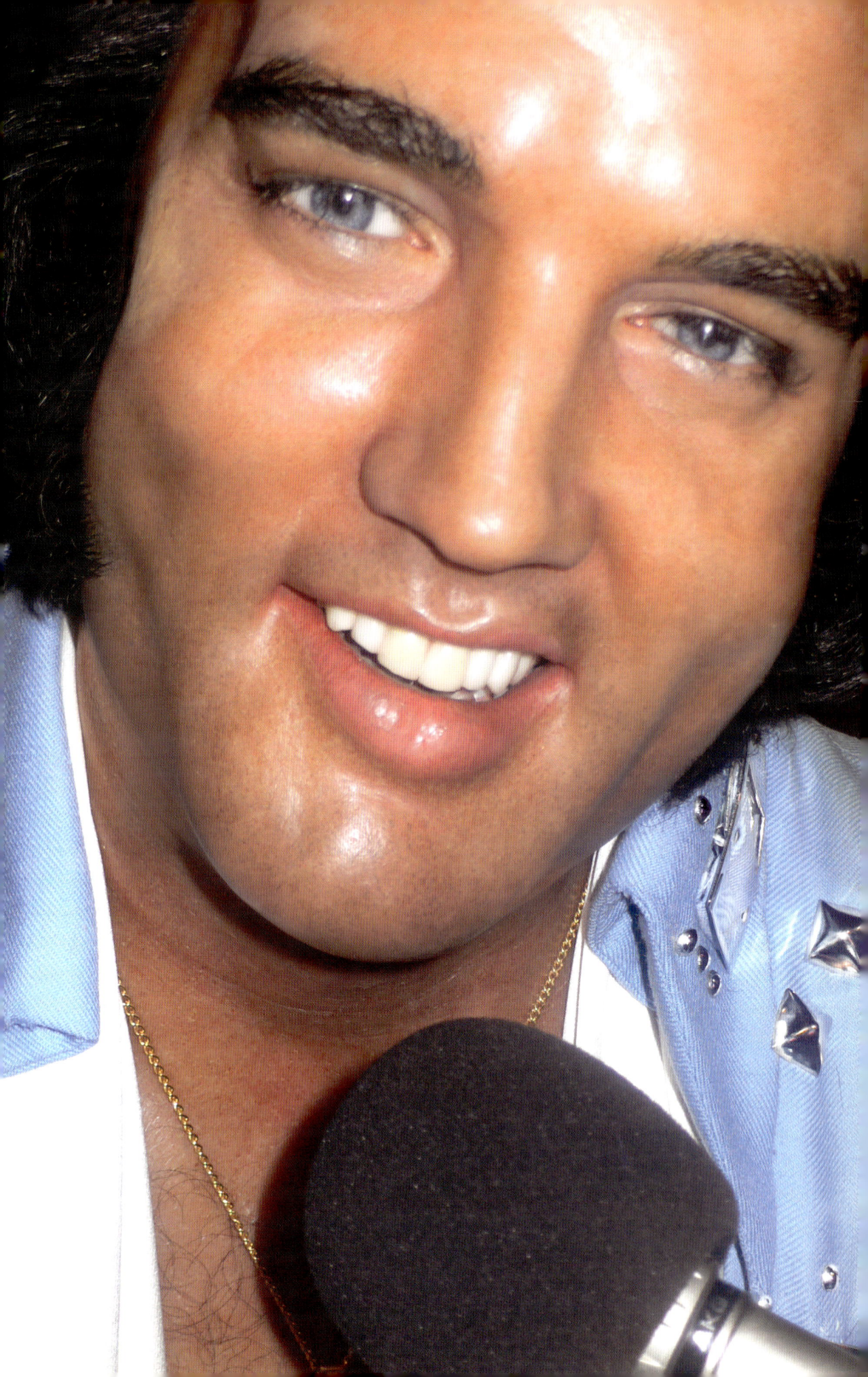

1. Elvis impersonator Kohki Ohyori of Japan.
2. The King's name in lights.
3. Elvis and Priscilla Presley posing near an airplane, 1967.
4. Kurt Russell as an Elvis impersonator and thief in *3000 Miles to Graceland*.
5. Ann-Margret and Elvis Presley in *Viva Las Vegas* (1964).
6. A scene in *Austin Powers: International Man of Mystery* (1997).
7. Kurt Russell, Christian Slater, Bokeem Woodbine, David Arquette, and Kevin Costner in the film *3000 Miles to Graceland* (2001).

(now the Las Vegas Hilton) which welcomed him with open arms and packed houses. In 1969, Presley kicked off his first four-week stint at the hotel's showroom, filling the fifteen-hundred-seat theater for two shows a night. This record-breaking engagement would be the start of a series of live concerts in Vegas, which sustained Presley until his death. He performed a staggering eight hundred shows at the International before officially leaving the building in 1976. Presley lived in the lap of Vegas luxury inside the hotel's five thousand-square-foot Imperial Suite on the thirtieth floor. He spent his days sleeping, his nights performing, and his downtime partying with transplanted members of his Memphis Mafia. It was here, in 1973, that Elvis and Priscilla agreed to separate. It was also here that Elvis reputedly shot out a television set with one of his many handguns; he apparently didn't like what performer Robert Goulet had to say on a talk show. As his life spiraled out of control, Presley hunkered down in Vegas, hoping to find happiness in the thousands of fans who had made the pilgrimage to see him, by this time overweight and sweat-soaked inside his jeweled wool jumpsuits.

Presley passed away in 1977 at the age of forty-two. But his music continues to echo throughout Vegas. Myriad Elvis impersonators make their living paying homage to the one musical icon that so encompassed the entertaining spirit of Las Vegas. While today you may not be able to see the King in concert, you can have him preside over your nuptials, or check him out in the seedy lounges of the smaller hotels. Better still, you can witness literally hundreds of incarnations of him—young, slim, and sexy, or side-burned, chunky, and sporting sunglasses—at the annual Elvis conventions. And you will likely always associate him, real or fake, with the city that set his soul on fire. Viva Las Vegas.

Elvis and Ann-Margret in *Viva Las Vegas* (1964).

Elvis in concert at the International Hotel, 1969.
Opposite: The Hard Rock Hotel, Las Vegas.

Marriage Capital

In 1939, socialite Ria Langham arrived in Las Vegas for six weeks, to wait out the required time for her quickie divorce—gambling, mingling, horseback riding, sailing, and even skiing at nearby Mount Charleston all the while. Her escapades as a pretty young divorcée made news around the county, and not solely due to her freewheeling mandated residency, but because her soon-to-be-ex-husband was none other than Clark Gable, the hottest star in Hollywood.

Gable was garnering his own press back home in the gossip pages, blatantly carrying on a very public extramarital affair with Carole Lombard, whom he would eventually marry. Yet it was Langham's brief stay in Vegas that caused a true marketing boon for the town, luring thousands of other unhappily marrieds to the desert to celebrate the demise of one of life's chapters and to kick off the next with a fresh attitude, and a merry roll of the dice. After all, six weeks of waiting for a divorce decree was far less than the standard six months. And doing so while shooting craps at a Vegas casino, basking poolside or waterskiing on Lake Mead was a far more pleasant way to pass the time.

Divorces in Vegas may have been on the rise in the 1940s, but quickie marriages had already caught on. As Nevada didn't require blood tests or waiting periods, couples came to Vegas by the thousands to get hitched in a hurry, without the hassle. The city has used every ploy to keep its unlikely existence afloat. When other states cracked down on some regulation or another, Vegas took it as a sign to loosen up. No wagering? Vegas set up tables. No liquor? Vegas opened backroom bars. Eventually Las Vegas even outlawed the need for ministers to be licensed through a particular church, thus allowing them to perform ceremonies whenever and wherever they so pleased. The twenty-four

Vegas is filled with dreamers. In this photo, a woman impersonates Marilyn Monroe.

1. Mickey Rooney, who was married four times by age 32, carries Elaine Mahnken over the threshold, 1953.
2. A neon sign promotes a wedding chapel.
3. An Elvis impersonator serenades newlyweds, 2004.
4. Marriage to go: a bride and groom at a drive-up chapel.
5. Frank Sinatra walks his daughter Nancy down the aisle at her wedding to teen star Tommy Sands, 1960.
6. Cupid's Wedding Chapel sign. Love and marriage are a winning combination in this town.
7. Sammy Davis Jr. cuts the cake with bride Loray White at the Sands Hotel, 1958.
8. A couple leaves their drive-through wedding at A Little White Wedding Chapel on motorbike.

hour mentality made tying the knot as easy as looking in the phone book. Soon chapels were popping up all over town, one-room buildings with an altar, a few pews, flowers, and a piano for "Here Comes the Bride."

Heading off to Vegas became the thing to do for spontaneous lovebirds looking for a rush. Celebrities hoping to avoid the glare of Hollywood's notorious paparazzi constantly snuck off to Vegas for covert nuptials. Frank Sinatra and Mia Farrow, Elvis Presley and Priscilla Beaulieu, Judy Garland, Brigitte Bardot, Tony Curtis, Joan Crawford, Jane Fonda and Roger Vadim, Paul Newman and Joanne Woodward, Bruce Willis and Demi Moore, Cindy Crawford and Richard Gere, and countless other stars all got hitched Vegas. And why not? Where else can you order an Elvis impersonator to perform your vows? Or rent a vintage pink Cadillac and swap rings in a drive-through ceremony? For their 2000 T-shirt-and-jeans nuptials at the Little Church of the West, Angelina Jolie and Billy Bob Thornton opted for the cheapest package on the chapel's à la carte wedding menu: $189 for the ceremony, a bouquet, and a few pictures. And an extra $29 for Angie's ring.

There are others, of course, with more extravagant tastes. One highroller husband reportedly forked over two-million-dollars for his bride's dream wedding at the Bellagio, complete with Petrossian caviar, Dom Perignon, and thousands of pink roses. Yet every couple, no matter their economic status, must go through the paperwork process at the Clark County Marriage License Bureau downtown. It's not a glamorous place, but it's open more hours than any bureau of its kind; until midnight on weekdays, and twenty-four-hours on weekends and holidays.

About 120,000 marriage licenses are doled out in Vegas each year. On Valentine's Day and New Year's Eve, couples can wait up to twelve hours at the Marriage Bureau on a line stretching around the block. But for those who do it, no matter the date—or the duration of their mariage—the phrase "We got married in Vegas" will stay with them for a lifetime.

Jayne Mansfield celebrates with a three tiered cake.

The Strip

In 1940, Highway 91 was a lonely stretch of road, leading out of bustling Los Angeles into what was essentially a no-man's-land, a barren desert of nothingness that eventually deposited travelers into downtown Las Vegas. Most of the bustle stayed within Vegas' city limits, Fremont Street to be exact. Gambling halls were growing in popularity, the Wild West theme was settling in nicely, and the area was gaining a steady following of visitors and business owners. California gambling sharks and casino operators were also flocking to Vegas, mainly because they had been chased out of Los Angeles, where the authorities were cracking down on illegal gaming. But in Vegas, well, these people contained a very special skill: they knew the business.

Thomas Hull, a respected California hotelier, was starting to pay attention to Las Vegas as well. A legit businessman, Hull already owned a handful of resorts in the Golden State and was looking for new action. He figured, and rightly so, that Vegas was in need of something to shake things up a bit. But instead of sniffing around downtown, Hull proceeded to buy 133 acres on Highway 91, which was not inside the city limits and was about three miles from the hoopla of Fremont Street. Even though he got the land at a steal, $150 per acre, or so the story goes, most people were sure that Hull was missing the mark. That he would even consider building not only a casino, but an actual resort hotel on this outlying land was incomprehensible.

However, Hull understood that the tourists who headed to Las Vegas from the West had to get there via Highway 91, as there was no other way into town—and they'd have to go by his new

In Las Vegas, only natural light distinguishes day from night.

Jon Favreau and Vince Vaughn as Mike Peters and Trent Walkers, bachelors who head to Vegas for a good time, in *Swingers* (1996).

property. So he set out to build something that would be almost impossible to pass by.

On April 3, 1941, the El Rancho opened its doors and the Las Vegas Strip was born. With sixty-five rooms and resort-style amenities, Hull's El Rancho suited a more moneyed clientele than the basic, sawdust-floored casino halls of downtown. There was a pool, a restaurant, retail shops, lush gardens, a health club, and even showgirls. The El Rancho gained popularity in an amazingly short time, and by 1942 it had company on Highway 91; the Last Frontier came to fruition in all its Old West glory, complete with a faux mining town and authentic covered wagons. The Last Frontier was actually the first casino resort and tourist attraction rolled into one, a trend that would boom over the next several decades. Today you can't build a casino without some sort of coexisting attraction—the two go hand-in-hand.

As for who gave the Strip its official title, that honor goes to Guy McAfee, a former LAPD cop turned notorious gambling magnate who fled to Las Vegas to ply his trade—one of the ousted Angelenos with plenty of work in Sin City. McAfee apparently still had a fondness for Los Angeles, and as hotels grew along Highway 91, he paid homage to the city's famed Sunset Strip by calling this new stretch of road "the Strip." The name stuck, McAfee made a bundle in Vegas, and the two Strips ultimately became very different entities.

Over the next several years, the Strip would become perhaps the most well-known main drag in America, if not the world. With almost nothing beyond the hotels and resorts that sprang up seemingly overnight, the Strip was a lonely but lively outcropping in the middle of the desert. Throughout the 1950s and 60s, resorts were opening one after another, most with Mob-backed financing, but spectacular in scale and scope nonetheless. Each wanted to

The hotel Paris Las Vegas, which boasts a half-scale replica of the Eiffel Tower and a neon sign in the shape of a Montgolfier balloon.

1. A police car stationed outside a burlesque club on the Strip in the 1940s.
2. The facade of the Paris Las Vegas at night.
3. Caesars Palace at night.
4. Johnny Depp as Raoul Duke in *Fear and Loathing in Las Vegas* (1998).
Following pages: The facade of the New York-New York Hotel & Casino.

outdo the last. The Desert Inn introduced a golf course, The Silver Slipper featured a convention hall, the Moulin Rouge was the first racially integrated hotel, the Sands boasted the most beautiful showgirls, Caesars Palace the most luxurious vacation experience, Circus Circus a fabulous adventure for the whole family. And on and on it went. If it could be dreamed, it could find a home on the Las Vegas Strip. Money, land, construction, and innovation—this was the recipe for success, the special language that could only be understood and acknowledged in Sin City. Tourists ate it up. There was something new and exciting with each hotel's grand opening. Celebrities, entertainers, and glamour girls from Hollywood were frequently spotted christening the tables in the casinos and the spotlights in the shows.

There was always something to do on the Strip, which overtook its downtown counterpart in a matter of a few years. Whereas you could merely duck in and out of a Fremont Street gambling hall for a few hours, on the Strip you could spend a weekend fully taken care of, without ever leaving your hotel. The Sahara, the Dunes, the Hacienda, the Riviera, the Tropicana—these spectacular places were havens of imaginary lifestyles, snippets of dreamworlds filled with fantasy, money, and the sweet hum of the most powerful air-conditioning systems ever invented. Comfortable, over-the-top, and with the largest "Come on in!" signage in the known world, these resorts changed the face of hospitality. The most incredible part? Las Vegas was still only in its infancy.

A colorful promotion for Las Vegas.

The infamous advertisement for the Crazy Girls revue.

An artistic rendering of the W Las Vegas Hotel, Casino, and Residences.

Howard Hughes

By 1936, mobsters had moved into Las Vegas, and decorum had moved out. All over town, the syndicate was skimming, running legit businessmen out of town and giving gentlemen gamblers a bad name. Fade in on a new chapter, starring Howard Hughes.

The movie mogul-cum-American eccentric rolled into town in the middle of the night on November 27 via private train, with big plans for Sin City. Before the sun was up, Hughes and his handful of henchmen were ensconced on the top two floors of the Desert Inn, occupying the property's prime high-roller suites and buying up at least ten days' worth of time. Hughes, by now a shut-in, obsessed with cleanliness, privacy, and his own bodily functions, lived alone on one floor, while his minions ran his business holdings on the floor below.

The setup worked well for a time. For Hughes, who wanted to escape California and establish a name for himself as a Las Vegas power player, the Desert Inn became a sanitized sanctuary, ground zero for the dealings that would change the face of the city outside its darkened windows. But little did anyone know that an overstayed welcome at one of Vegas' most popular hotels would morph into the largest takeover in modern urban history. Less than a month after Hughes's arrival, Desert Inn owner Moe Dalitz was ready to remove the welcome mat. The holiday season was looming, and Dalitz had full books; the DI's best clients were slated for Hughes's rooms. Undaunted, and not one to budge, Hughes bought the Desert Inn.

Thus began his legendary buying binge, and the onslaught of legends that exist about the mysterious mogul to this day. In two years time, Hughes snatched up the Castaways, the New Frontier, the Landmark, the Sands, and the Silver Slipper—the latter because its

Howard Hughes in his aviator gear, 1936.

bright, rotating sign shined through Hughes' hotel window; hence, he bought the property and adjusted the glare.

Hughes would also purchase thousands of acres of land, office space, even the local CBS affiliate, just so he could select late-night movies that suited his fancy. Hughes's helpers would phone in messages to the station, asking that films pick up where he'd fallen asleep the night before. Rumor has it he once requested that the local anchorman smile more. And locals still talk about his request for 350 gallons of a discontinued flavor of Baskin-Robbins ice cream, which was specially shipped from Los Angeles to Las Vegas. Still, no one could ever say they actually saw Hughes, but his growing monopoly essen-tially ran the Mob out of town and started the era of casinos run by organized corporate entities. Under his brief reign, rules were obeyed, shysters were denied, and tourists happily spent dollar after dollar under the neon glow of Hughes's properties. And then on November 5, 1970, nearly four years to the day from his unannounced arrival, he disappeared. It would be weeks before anyone knew he had gone.

Howard Hughes, ca. 1930s.

1. The control tower at WIlliam P. Hobby Airport, Houston, Texas, 2000. Hughes was responsible for several improvements to its construction in 1938.
2. "Welcome home, Howard" sign, erected in February 1972 during a lawsuit against Hughes.
3. Hughes dancing with Ginger Rogers, ca. 1930s.
4. Advertisement for Hughes' *The Outlaw*, starring Jane Russell, (1946).
5. A scene from *The Aviator* (2004), starring Leonardo DiCaprio as Howard Hughes.
6. A hobo hitches a ride on an airplane by holding onto landing iron.
7. Hughes with Ginger Rogers, 1933.

THE MUSIC HALLS *get the big ones!*

WHAT ARE THE TWO GREAT REASONS FOR JANE RUSSELL'S RISE TO STARDOM?....

SHE'S DARING AND EXCITING

IN HOWARD HUGHES' THRILLING PRODUCTION

The Showgirl

If ever there was an ambassador for Las Vegas, it is the showgirl. Leggy and lithe, the showgirl symbolizes the seduction of Sin City. She incites fantasies and transports her audience into the world they came to Vegas to discover. Her talent is that special glide, the sexual stage prowl which enables hips to thrust forward, necks to extend, and shoulders to be pushed back, all without looking the slightest bit awkward. It's a trick honed in the city's showrooms, dating back to the days of Donn Arden's *Lido de Paris* at the Stardust in 1958.

Along with entertainers and Hollywood, the 1950s brought an onslaught of showgirls to the venues along the Strip. These glittering objects of desire were like mannequins come to life. Most would mingle and socialize between shows, flirting with the big-time gamblers and rubbing elbows with celebrities and headliners. The image of a dancer on the arm of Frank Sinatra in the Sands hotel lounge had young women across America dreaming of a showgirl career in Vegas.

But what would Vegas be without excess and decadence? So, naturally, the city pushed the envelope, scouting topless girls to lead chorus lines, the standard in France, but still a shocking concept in America. Harold Minsky was the first to have his showgirls doff their tops in *Minsky's Follies* in 1957 at the Desert Inn. The move again landed Vegas on the map, garnering all sorts of publicity for the booming casino industry, and for the "extras" that a player was privy to when he made the trip to the desert. After all, a half-naked woman wasn't something one saw on the streets of Kansas or Iowa. To this day, Donn Arden's *Jubilee!* at Bally's and the *Folies Bergere* at the Tropicana, two of the longest-running showgirl productions

A showgirl in a white bikini and accessories.

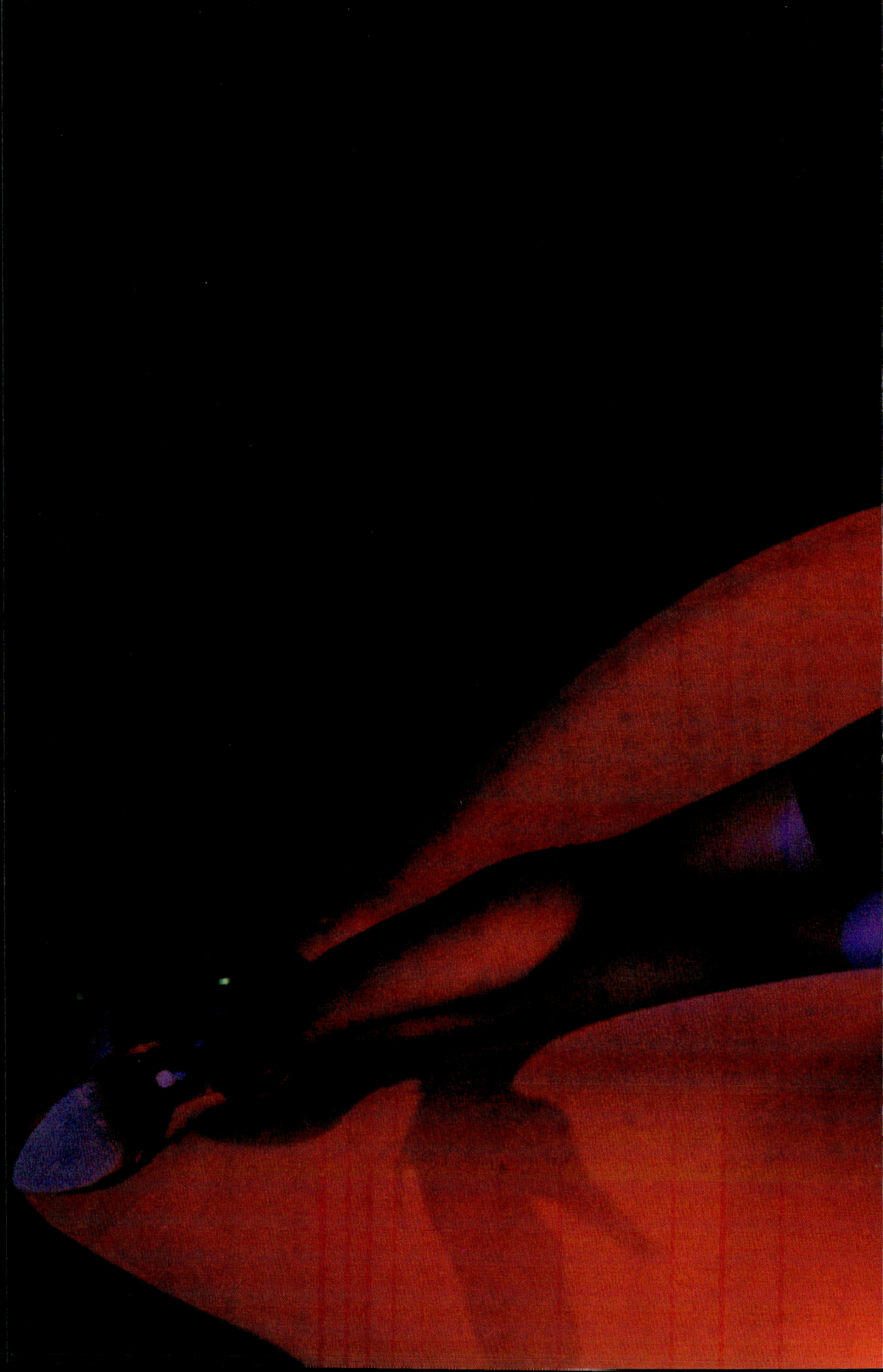

A Crazy Horse dancer in *La Femme,* at the MGM Grand Hotel.

(and the only two full-scale revues left on the Strip) still have topless shows each night.

It must be said that the allure of the showgirl is surprisingly more about grace and charm than nudity and vulgarity. Oddly, in a town with accents so bold only neon could make them any more obvious, there is a tastefulness to the showgirl. She is neither lewd nor lascivious, yet there is a confidence in her seduction that renders the naked aspect completely devoid of degradation.

As much as the showgirl was seen as fluff for casino patrons, she is still a one-of-a-kind treasure, and she is now officially a Las Vegas endangered species. The onslaught of magicians, musicals, and Cirque du Soleil has rendered the showgirl all but extinct. With the exception of *Jubilee!, Folies Bergere,* and *Splash!* at the Riviera, there are no full-production showgirl revues, at least in the original vein. The MGM Grand imported the topless yet modern *La Femme* from Paris, courtesy of the famed Crazy Horse, and a few other hotels have topless productions, but the focus is more on sex than the grace and elegance of the dancers themselves. There is hardly poise involved in a rock-and-roll-based show titled *Erocktica* (at the Rio). Perhaps it's just a sign of the times—changing tastes, ever-evolving entertainment trends. Or it could be the grueling work: the life of a showgirl is hardly the glitzy dream portrayed onstage. To this day, most dancers are re-auditioned approximately every six months to ensure they continue to meet the physical requirements: height, weight, proportionality, and dance skill. If a showgirl has put on pounds, she's likely given the boot.

And no matter the physical strain, the showgirl is required to make the burden of rhinestones, feathers, and ostentatious Bob Mackie costumes appear effortless. Thirty-five pound headdresses are often lowered onto the dancers' heads just before the women take the stage, as the headdresses are simply too big to fit through

Three showgirls in Minsky's Follies at the Dunes Hotel pose in *Arabian Nights*-themed costumes. ca. 1960.

Nightclub dancer Maria Corvier (Cyd Charisse) performs her "Frankie and Johnny" routine in the 1956 comedic romance *Meet Me in Las Vegas*.

the dressing room door, and too bulky to attach in the common dressing area. At *Jubilee!*, three massive elevators bring the multimillion-dollar sets to and from the main stage, quite a feat considering the show encompasses everything from the tale of Samson and Delilah to the sinking of the *Titanic,* which meets its doom twice a night. All the while, showgirls (and showboys) sidestep the chaos in perfectly groomed hair, expertly applied makeup, and three-inch heels.

Yet no matter the fate of these illustrious productions, there will surely always be a place in Las Vegas for the showgirl. The image alone has been used countless times in marketing campaigns, promotional videos, even reality television. At every major Las Vegas event, you will find one of these ladies, dressed in full-feathered finery, complete with mile-long false eyelashes and lacquered lips. She will travel the world to encapsulate the fantasy of Las Vegas, a living apparition of the dreamworld that exists deep in the Nevada desert.

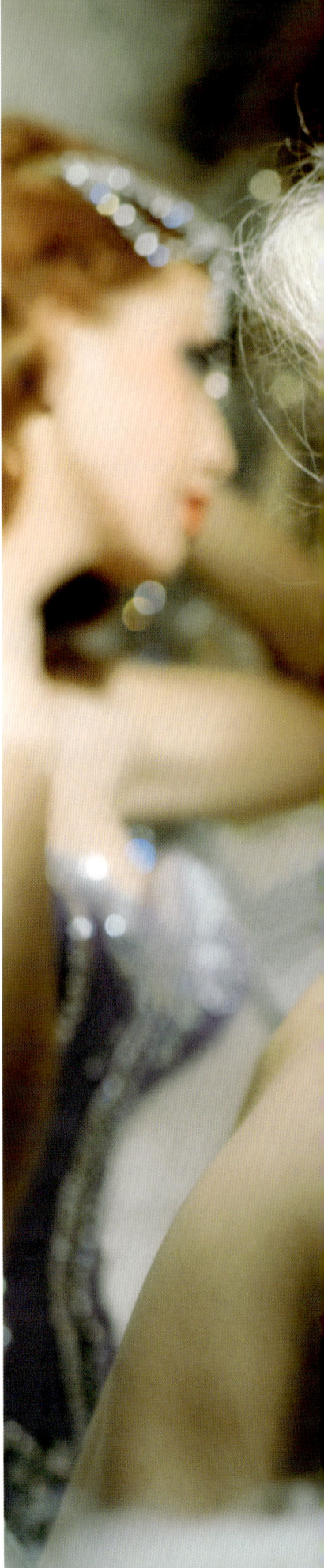

Showgirls primping before their performance.

Hotels

A Las Vegas hotel is much more than a place to spend the night. Whereas a property's proximity to the major sites, exemplary service, luxurious rooms, and fine dining are usually enough to satisfy discerning guests in other tourist towns, visitors to Vegas often choose their accommodations based on such features as, say, an on-premise roller coaster, an erupting volcano, or even a water canal. In Vegas, the hotels are what people come to see, and not just where they stay.

The year 1966 marked the opening of Caesars Palace, an ornate, Grecian-inspired white monolith. Owner and creator Jay Sarno dreamed of a place where guests could feel as though they were Greco-Roman VIPs. Built for an astounding $24 million, Sarno and his palace set the bar for the vacationing experience. Over the years, dozens of the world's top entertainment acts would play the famed Circus Maximus showroom, and leading boxers made Caesars the spot to hold the big fights. Sarno was so intent on making the visitor feel at home when they came to his hotel, he dropped the apostrophe from Caesars, thus relinquishing a Caesars-only hold on the place and allowing everyone to partake of this royal lifestyle.

In 1968, Sarno once again created something new and inspired with the hot-pink fantasyland Circus Circus. A family-oriented fun house on steroids, Circus Circus was filled from top to bottom with three-ring acts, trapeze artists, arcades and of course, a full-scale casino. Sarno's astute innovation was a venue where both parents and children could spend money simulataneously.

The sunlit exterior of the Wynn Hotel.

The penthouse suite at the Bellagio.

1. Winged statues at Caesars Palace Hotel and Casino.
2. Four sunbathers lounge on leopard-print rafts at a Vegas hotel, 1968.
3. The interior of Caesars Palace.
4. The pool cabanas at The Mirage, complete with nightly volcanic eruptions.
5. A guestmobile at the Sands Hotel, ca. 1950s.
6. The lobby of the Wynn.

Sarno was just one of a handful of visionaries who would soon change Las Vegas forever. Mogul Kirk Kerkorian built the biggest hotel in Las Vegas when the 2,100-room MGM Grand opened in 1973. Kerkorian was a serious player, and he was also a risk taker. When the old MGM Grand almost burned to the ground in a fire in 1980, Kerkorian boldly reopened the hotel, and then sold the property a few years later to Bally's. But he held on to the name, and when the second incarnation of the MGM Grand opened in 1993, it cost over $1 billion, and at 5,044 rooms was the largest hotel in the world.

Steve Wynn would also make his mark in Las Vegas, starting with The Mirage, which opened in 1989 right next door to Caesars Palace. Wynn, however, saw an even bigger picture than Sarno and Kerkorian: he dreamed in Technicolor. His vision for The Mirage included insanely luxe high-roller villas for his best casino customers, a special habitat for dolphins, a multimillion-dollar showroom for his headliners, Siegfried & Roy (as well as for their big cats!), and a multitude of restaurants, bars, and entertainment venues, including a rainforest and an active volcano. Wynn

A lifeguard on-duty at Caesars Palace, 1982.

knew, long before his other counterparts did, that his guests wanted a complete experience. His gamble on Siegfried & Roy, for example, changed the face of entertainment in Las Vegas. Whereas pre-Wynn it was pretty much understood that entertainment was not a financial gain for a property, post-Wynn entertainment became a huge part of the overall success of modern day casinos. All around, The Mirage was an instantaneous moneymaker. Steve Wynn became a legend.

The Mirage was the model for every elaborate property that followed on the Strip, in rapid succession. Treasure Island was pirate-themed. The Excalibur was a medieval wonderland. The Luxor, a nod to the pyramids, complete with the brightest beam of light in the world. And when the themes ran dry, casino entrepreneurs and corporations literally turned to other cities for inspiration. Soon there was New York–New York, Paris, the Venetian, and the Bellagio. A walk up and down the Strip became a trippy tour of the rest of the world, albeit a far more kitschy, vulgar, and humorous excursion.

Today the Las Vegas Strip is still the spectacle of innovation and brilliance that it was sixty years ago, only now the sky's truly the limit. On the drawing board, the Strip continues to bulge, with condominium proposals, sparkling new additions to Wynn Las Vegas and the Venetian, the MGM Mirage's planned $8 billion CityCenter, the W Las Vegas, the Cosmopolitan, and more. Highway 91 has morphed into the one street in the world that needs no introduction.

The curved escalator inside the Forum Shops at Caesars Palace.

1. The exclusive villas at the Wynn.
2. The hotel reception desk at the MGM Grand.
3. A replica of the sphinx and pyramids at the Luxor.
4. *Fiore di Como,* the glass ceiling sculpture in the lobby of the Bellagio, by Dale Chihuly.
5. Gondoliers at the Venetian.
6. The turrets of the Excalibur.

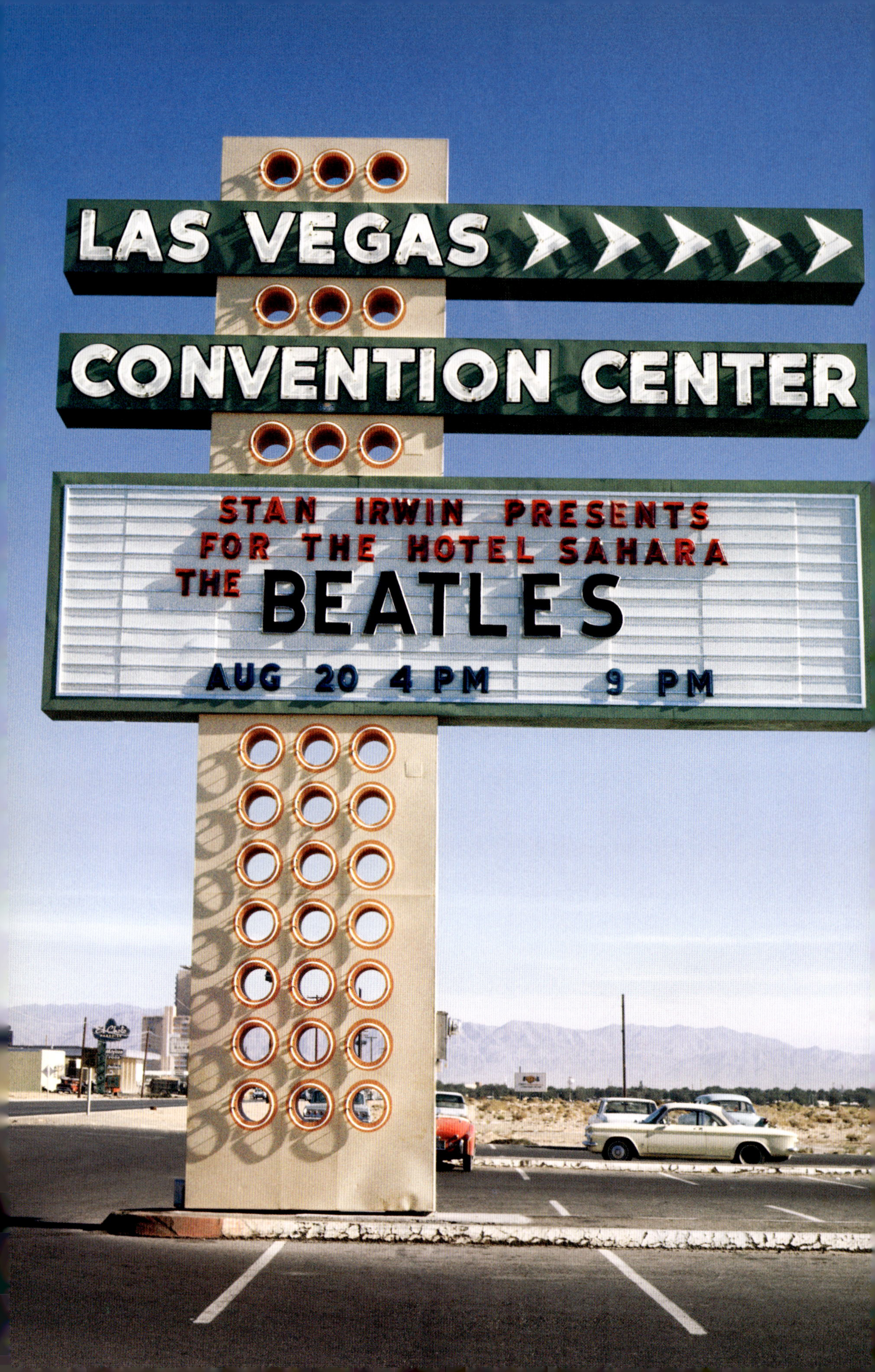
LAS VEGAS
CONVENTION CENTER
STAN IRWIN PRESENTS
FOR THE HOTEL SAHARA
THE BEATLES
AUG 20 4 PM 9 PM

Entertainment

Every night in Las Vegas, the curtain goes up on a fascinating array of entertainment. From the ubiquitous Vegas lounge acts to the multimillion-dollar Cirque du Soleil spectaculars, the Las Vegas Strip is home to a delicious selection of the hippest, hottest and most ingenious productions of our time.

True, Vegas has gone through more than a few entertainment metamorphoses to get to its current post; the showgirls, the stand-up comics, the Rat Pack, Elvis Presley, Wayne Newton, Siegfried & Roy, and on and on. However, with each passing phase—and some would last for more than a decade—Las Vegas built itself into the "Entertainment Capital of the World," no small feat considering that the talent levels sometimes run the gamut from so-so to staggering. What started as a benign way to entertain antsy gamblers when the tables were slow, entertainment in Las Vegas is now an enormous part of the city's economic structure, adding a significant boost to a hotel's bottom line. That was not always the case. In the early days, entertainment was largely a financially disappointing venture for most properties, it was a sideshow to the headlining act, which was always, always the casino.

But the amplified evolution of Las Vegas as a city, a vacation destination, and a wonder of the world meant that entertainment would have to step up eventually. And step up it did. Stars like Liberace, who would redefine schmaltzy glitz and glamour, became synonymous with Las Vegas. A showman through and through, Liberace was everything the town was about—lights, costumes, and plenty of fantasy. In the 1970s, Liberace set the bar for another notable trait: his salary. Reaching into the hundreds of thousands per week at the

A marquee announcing the performance of the Beatles in Las Vegas, 1964.

Boxing promoter Don King with Mike Tyson after Tyson beat James "Bonecrusher" Smith in a heavyweight title fight on March 7, 1987.

Mohammed Ali prepares for his world heavyweight title match with heavyweight champion Larry Holmes in Las Vegas, 1980.

Evander Holyfield at Madame Tussauds wax museum.

Mohammed Ali with friend Howard Bingham in 1978.

Las Vegas Hilton, Liberace's lucrative deal lured other acts to town. Elvis Presley took a cue from the sequined entertainer, as did illusionists Siegfried & Roy.

Siegfried & Roy set a benchmark when they opened at Steve Wynn's new Mirage Hotel in 1989. It was the first time a hotel spent millions (approximately $40 million) on a showroom spectacle. Of course, other property owners thought Wynn was signing up for a losing proposition, but, as would prove to be the case for the next several years, he was spot-on. Siegfried & Roy fast became a huge profit boon for Wynn and The Mirage, drawing literally thousands of visitors each year. Soon it was clear that entertainment was well worth a substantial investment. Other hotels would follow suit, thanks to the trailblazing phenomenon that was Siegfried & Roy.

Their phantasmagoric production was a nightly sellout. Their illusions were bolstered by their cadre of big cats and their flair for excessive special effects. Siegfried & Roy would become legends, defining entertainment in Las Vegas and providing a singular experience that could only be found on the Strip. The duo performed at The Mirage for thirteen years, until October 2003, when Roy Horn was seriously injured by one of his tigers during a live show.

Cirque du Soleil eventually filled the vacancy at The Mirage in 2006, completely revamping the theater to open *LOVE,* a musical adventure featuring acrobatics and dance, set to the songs of the Beatles. The Cirque conglomerate now encompasses five shows on the Strip, including *KA,* at the MGM Grand. When Cirque overhauled the theater to make room for that production, the total bill came to $165 million, making *KA's* the most expensive showroom in the world.

Yet before there was Cirque, there were many other headliners and acts that would set up shop on the Strip. From Liza Minelli to Shecky Greene, performers of all shapes and sizes flocked to get a few

Tina Turner performing live, 1975.

Wrestlers throw salt to purify the ring at the Grand Sumo Championship at the Mandalay Bay Resort and Casino, 2005.

dates at one of the major hotels. At present, A-list singers and comedians still book Vegas gigs a few times a year, if only for the loose crowds and easy money.

Celine Dion kicked off a new trend in 2003, when she opened in *A New Day...* at the $90 million Colosseum theater at Caesars Palace. By performing in Las Vegas in a permanent venue, Dion brought the audience to her, allowing for a somewhat "normal" homelife with her family in an opulent home in a Vegas suburb. Dion could get off the road, spend the day with her husband and son, and make a mint in the process. Dion's success at Caesars spawned similar deals with Elton John, Jerry Seinfeld, and Barry Manilow, who took up semi-permanent residency at the Las Vegas Hilton. All of these performers overlooked the stigma of Sin City—which is commonly frowned upon by cultural snobs and sophisticates—in order to embrace the neon and all it has to offer.

A trip to Las Vegas almost requires a show of some sort for most of today's tourists. And the selection can't be beat. On any given night, the medley of shows, headliners, and visiting rock bands is stupefying. Yet there are still true nuggets of the Vegas entertainment of yesteryear, from the feathered showgirl headdresses at *Jubilee!* to the Rat Pack tribute show at the Greek Isles, to the ultimate lounge lizard, Cook E. Jarr. Modern extravaganzas such as Blue Man Group and a retooled *Phantom of the Opera,* both at the Venetian, are finding footing as well.

There is something for every genre of fan, be it country, pop, comedy, torch, or Broadway. Las Vegas will likely forever hold the title of Entertainment Capital of the World, as long as the curtains continue to rise on the most beguiling and captivating productions audiences have ever seen.

A performer at the opening of the Bellagio, home of Cirque du Soleil's *O,* 1998.

1. Siegfried & Roy.
2. Louis Armstrong at Madame Tussauds.
3. Marilyn Monroe at Madame Tussauds.
4. Liza Minelli at Madame Tussauds.
5. Celine Dion after the premiere of her show *A New Day...* at Caesars Colosseum, 2003
6. Elton John at *The Red Piano* premiere, 2004.
Following pages: An aerial view of the Strip at night.

LAS VEGAS GUIDE
HOTELS

BELLAGIO
3600 Las Vegas Blvd. South
702 693 7111
www.bellagio.com

CAESARS PALACE
3570 Las Vegas Blvd. South
800 851 1703
www.caesarspalace.com

CIRCUS CIRCUS
2880 Las Vegas Blvd. South
702 650 3499

FOUR SEASONS
3960 Las Vegas Blvd. South
702 632 5000
www.fourseasons.com

GREEN VALLEY RANCH
2300 Paseo Verde Drive
702 617 7777
www.greenvalleyranchresort.com

HARD ROCK HOTEL & CASINO
4455 Paradise Road
800 693 7625
www.hardrockhotel.com

LAS VEGAS HILTON
3000 South Paradise Road
Las Vegas, NV 89109
702 946 9200

LUXOR
3900 Las Vegas Blvd. South
702 262 4000
www.luxor.com

MANDALAY BAY
3950 Las Vegas Blvd. South
702 632 7777
877 632 7800
www.mandalaybay.com

MGM GRAND
3799 Las Vegas Blvd. South
877 880 0880
www.mgmgrand.com

THE MIRAGE
3400 Las Vegas Blvd. South
702 791 7111
www.mirage.com

MONTE CARLO
3770 Las Vegas Blvd. South
702 730 7777
www.montecarlo.com

PALMS
4321 West Flamingo Road
702 942 7777
www.palms.com

PARIS LAS VEGAS
3655 Las Vegas Blvd. South
877 796 2096
www.parislasvegas.com

PLATINUM HOTEL AND SPA
211 E. Flamingo Road
Las Vegas, NV 89169
702 369 2354

RED ROCK CASINO RESORT AND SPA
11011 West Charleston Blvd.
Las Vegas, NV 89135
702 797 7777
www.redrocklasvegas.com

THE RITZ-CARLTON
1610 Lake Las Vegas Pkwy.
702 567 4700
www.ritzcarlton.com

STRATOSPHERE
2000 Las Vegas Blvd. South
702 380 7777
www.stratospherehotel.com

TREASURE ISLAND
3300 Las Vegas Blvd. South
702 894 7111
www.treasureisland.com

WYNN LAS VEGAS
3131 Las Vegas Blvd. South
702 770 7100
www.wynnlasvegas.com

Artistic rendering of a W Hotel Suite.

ENTERTAINMENT

SHOWS

CELINE DION
The Colosseum: Caesars Palace
3570 Las Vegas Blvd. South
877 423 5463
www.celinedion.com

DANNY GANS
Danny Gans Theatre: The Mirage
3400 Las Vegas Blvd. South
702 792 7600
www.dannygans.com

DAVID COPPERFIELD
Hollywood Theatre: MGM Grand
3799 Las Vegas Blvd. South
866 807 4697
www.mgmgrand.com

ELTON JOHN
The Colosseum: Caesars Palace
3570 Las Vegas Blvd. South
877 274 3463
www.eltonjohn.com

JUBILEE!
Jubilee! Theatre: Bally's
3645 Las Vegas Blvd. South
702 492 3960
www.ballys.com

KÀ CIRQUE DU SOLEIL
KÀ Theatre: MGM Grand
3799 Las Vegas Blvd. South
702 492 5960
www.cirquedusoleil.com

LE RÊVE
Wynn Theater: Wynn Las Vegas
3131 Las Vegas Blvd. South
866 807 4697
www.wynnlasvegas.com

LOVE: THE LEGACY OF THE BEATLES
BY CIRQUE DU SOLEIL: The Mirage
3400 Las Vegas Blvd. South
702 792 7777
www.cirquedusoleil.com

"O" CIRQUE DU SOLEIL
Bellagio
3600 Las Vegas Blvd. South
702 693 7722
www.bellagio.com

SIGHTSEEING

KYLE CANYON
Head North on US 95. Take US 95 north 6 miles past the Santa Fe Hotel to State Route 157. Turn left (west) and continue for 17 miles into Kyle Canyon.

COLD CREEK
Continue on US 95, 21 miles past State Route 157 to Cold Creek Road. Turn left (west) and drive 16 miles until the road ends at Bonanza Trailhead.

LAKE MEAD
30 miles southeast of Las Vegas.
702 293 8907
www.riverlakes.com/lakemead.htm

RED ROCK CANYON
About 15 miles northwest of the Strip. Take Charleston Road west from I-15.
702 515 5367
www.redrockcanyonlv.org

HOOVER DAM
30 miles southeast of Las Vegas. US 93 at the Nevada-Arizona border.
702 597 5970
www.usbr.gov/lc/hooverdam

DOLPHIN HABITAT AT THE MIRAGE
3400 Las Vegas Blvd. South
702 791 7980

ETHEL M. CHOCOLATE FACTORY AND
BOTANICAL CACTUS GARDENS
2 Cactus Garden Drive
Henderson, NV
888 987 3456
www.ethelm.com

FOUNTAINS OF BELLAGIO
3600 Las Vegas Blvd. South
702 693 7111
www.bellagio.com

SHARK REEF at Mandalay Bay
3950 Las Vegas Blvd. South
877 632 7800
www.mandalaybay.com

WILDLIFE HABITAT
Flamingo Las Vegas
3555 Las Vegas Blvd. South
702 733 3111
www.flamingolasvegas.com

Marquees from an assortment of shows.

BARS &CLUBS

BEAUTY BAR
517 Fremont Street
Las Vegas, NV 89101
702 598 1965

BODY ENGLISH
4455 Paradise Road
702 693 4000
www.bodyenglish.com

EMPIRE BALLROOM
3765 Las Vegas Blvd. South
Las Vegas, NV 89109
702 737 7375

GHOSTBAR
Palms
4321 West Flamingo Road
702.492.3960
800 851 1703
www.palms.com

HOUSE OF BLUES
Mandalay Bay
3950 Las Vegas Blvd. South
702 632 7600
www.hob.com

JET
The Mirage
3400 Las Vegas Blvd. South
702 792 7900
www.mirage.com

KRAVE
Desert Passage Mall
3663 Las Vegas Blvd. South
702 836 0830
www.kravelasvegas.com

LIGHT
Bellagio
3600 Las Vegas Blvd. South
702 693 8300
www.bellagio.com

MIX LOUNGE
The Rooftop at Mandalay Bay
3950 Las Vegas Blvd. South
877 632 7800
www.thehotelatmandalaybay.com

PURE
Caesars Palace
3570 Las Vegas Blvd. South
702 731 7873
www.caesars.com

RA
Luxor
3900 Las Vegas Blvd. South
702 262 4949
www.ralv.com

RAIN
4321 West Flamingo Road
800 670 6423
www.palms.com

RISQUÉ
Paris Las Vegas
3655 Las Vegas Blvd. South, Suite 3
702 492 3960
866 80SHOWS
www.parislasvegas.com

RUMJUNGLE
Mandalay Bay
3950 Las Vegas Blvd. South
702 632 7777
www.thehotelatmandalaybay.com

TABU
3799 Las Vegas Blvd. South
702 891 7183
www.mgmgrand.com

TANGERINE
Treasure Island Hotel & Casino
3300 Las Vegas Blvd. South
702 492 3960
www.treasureisland.com

TAO
The Venetian
3355 Las Vegas Blvd. South
702 388 8588
www.taorestaurant.com

TRYST
Wynn Las Vegas
3131 Las Vegas Blvd. South
702 770 3375
www.wynnlasvegas.com

VOODOO LOUNGE
Rio
3700 West Flamingo Road
702 777 7800
www.riovegasnights.com

WEST WING BAR
3799 Las Vegas Blvd. South
Las Vegas, NV 89109
702 891 8521

STRIP CLUBS
CHEETAHS
2112 Western Avenue
702 384 0074
www.cheetahsnv.com

CLUB PARADISE
4416 Paradise Road
702 734 7990
www.clubparadise.net

CRAZY HORSE TOO
2476 South Industrial Road
702 382 8003
www.crazyhorsetoo.com

OLYMPIC GARDEN
531 Las Vegas Blvd. South
800 593 6423
www.ogvegas.com

PLAYBOY CLUB
Palms
4321 West Flamingo Road
702 942 7777
www.playboyclub.com

SAPPHIRE
3025 South Industrial Road
800 593 6423
www.sapphirelasvegas.com

SPEARMINT RHINO
3340 South Highland Drive
702 796 3600
www.spearmintrhino.com

SPORTS AND SPAS

SPAS

BATHHOUSE SPA AT MANDALAY BAY
Mandalay Bay
3950 Las Vegas Blvd. South
877 632 9636
www.thehotelatmandalaybay.com

CANYON RANCH SPA AND CLUB
The Venetian
3355 Las Vegas Blvd. South
877 220 2688
www.venetian.com

GRAND SPA AND HEALTH CLUB
MGM Grand
3799 Las Vegas Blvd. South
702 891 3077
www.mgmgrand.com

QUA BATHS & SPA AT CAESARS PALACE
3570 Las Vegas Blvd. South
866 690 6270
www.harrahs.com

SONA MEDSPA OF LAS VEGAS
4730 South Fort Apache Road, Suite 150
702 367 7662
www.sonamedspa.com

THE SPA BELLAGIO
3600 Las Vegas Blvd. South
702 693 7111
www.bellagio.com

THE SPA AT THE FOUR SEASONS
3960 Las Vegas Blvd. South
702 632 5000
www.fourseasons.com

SPA VITA DI LAGO
The Ritz-Carlton, Lake Las Vegas
1610 Lake Las Vegas Pkwy.
702 567 4700
www.ritzcarlton.com

SPA AT WYNN LAS VEGAS
Wynn Las Vegas
3131 Las Vegas Blvd. South
702 770 7100
www.wynnlasvegas.com

TRUEFITT & HILL: A GENTLEMAN'S BARBERSHOP
3500 Las Vegas Blvd. South
866 714 1115
www.truefittandhill.com

GOLF

ANGEL PARK GOLF CLUB
100 Rampart Blvd. South
702 254 4653
www.angelpark.com

ANTHEM COUNTRY CLUB
1 Grosse Pointe Place
702 914 3000
www.anthemclubliving.com

BALI HAI GOLF CLUB
5160 Las Vegas Blvd. South
888 427 6678
www.balihaigolfclub.com

CLUBSPORT GREEN VALLEY
2100 Olympic Avenue
702 454 6000
www.clubsports.com

DESERT PINES GOLF CLUB
3415 East Bonanza Road
702 450 8000
www.desert-pines-golf-club.com

DESERT ROSE GOLF COURSE
5483 Club House Drive
702 431 4653
www.desert-rose-golf-course.com

JW MARRIOTT GOLF
221 North Rampart Blvd.
877 869 8777
www.jwlasvegasresort.com

LAS VEGAS PAIUTE GOLF RESORT
10325 Nu-Wav Kaiv Blvd.
702 658 1400
www.lvpaiutegolf.com

THE LEGACY GOLF CLUB
130 Par Excellence Drive
702 897 2108
www.thelegacygc.com

REFLECTION BAY GOLF CLUB
Lake Las Vegas Resort
75 Montelago Blvd.
702 740 4653
www.lakelasvegas.com

ROYAL LINKS GOLF CLUB
5995 Vegas Valley Drive
702 450 8123
www.royal-links-golf-club.com

The sixth hole of the Wynn golf course.

RESTAURANTS

ALEX
Wynn Las Vegas
3131 Las Vegas Blvd. South
888 320 7110
www.wynnlasvegas.com

ANDRE'S FRENCH RESTAURANT
401 Sixth Street South
702 385 5016
www.andrelv.com

AUREOLE
Mandalay Bay
3950 Las Vegas Blvd. South
702 632 7401
www.aureolelv.com

BARTOLOTTA RISTORANTE DI MARE
Wynn Las Vegas
3131 Las Vegas Blvd. South
702 770 3305

BOUCHON
The Venetian
3355 Las Vegas Blvd. South
702 414 6200
www.frenchlaundry.com

CHARLIE PALMER STEAK
Four Seasons Hotel
3960 Las Vegas Blvd. South
702 632 5120
www.charliepalmersteaklv.com

DANIEL BOULUD BRASSERIE
Wynn Las Vegas
3131 Las Vegas Blvd. South
702 770 3463
www.wynnlasvegas.com

FIN
The Mirage
3400 Las Vegas Blvd. South
702.791.7223
www.themirage.com

FIX
Bellagio
3600 Las Vegas Blvd. South
877 234 6358
www.bellagio.com

GALLAGHER'S STEAKHOUSE
New York - New York
3790 Las Vegas Blvd. South
Las Vegas, NV, 89109
702 740 6450

JOEL ROBUCHON
MGM Grand
3799 Las Vegas Blvd. South
702 891 7925
www.robuchon.com

LITTLE BUDDHA
Palms
4321 West Flamingo Road
702 942 7778
www.littlebuddhalasvegas.com

NOBU
Hard Rock Hotel & Casino
4455 Paradise Road
702 693 5090
www.noburestaurants.com

PIERO'S
355 Convention Center Drive
702 369 2305
www.pieroscuisine.com

PRIME STEAKHOUSE
Bellagio
3600 Las Vegas Blvd. South
877 234 6358
www.bellagio.com

SOCIAL HOUSE
Treasure Island
3300 Las Vegas Blvd. South
800.944.7444
www.treasureisland.com

SW STEAKHOUSE
Wynn Las Vegas
3131 Las Vegas Blvd. South
702 770 3463
www.wynnlasvegas.com

TAO
The Venetian
3355 Las Vegas Blvd. South
702 492 3960
www.taorestaurant.com

THE TILLERMAN
2245 East Flamingo Road
Las Vegas, NV, 89119
702 731 4036

WING LEI
Wynn Las Vegas
3131 Las Vegas Blvd. South
702 770 3388
www.wynnlasvegas.com

Prime steakhouse at the Bellagio.

LIBERACE MUSEUM
1775 East Tropicana Avenue
702 798 5595

MADAME TUSSAUDS
3377 Las Vegas Blvd. South
Suite 2001
Las Vegas
NV 89109
702 862 7800
www.mtvegas.com

TOURS
SUNDANCE HELICOPTERS
McCarran International Airport
5596 Haven Street
702 736 0606
www.helicoptour.com

PAPILLON HELICOPTERS LAS VEGAS
McCarran Executive Terminal
275 East Tropicana Avenue, Suite 155
702 736 7243
www.papillon.com

LAS VEGAS HELICOPTER INC.
888 779 0800
www.lvhelicopters.com

PINK JEEP TOURS
3629 W. Hacienda Avenue
702 895 6777
www.pinkjeeptours.com

RICHARD PETTY DRIVING EXPERIENCE
6775 Speedway Blvd.
Suite D106
702 643 4343

COWBOY TRAIL RIDES
702 948 7061
www.cowboytrailrides.com

FLORISTS
A FRENCH BOUQUET FLOWER SHOPS
3265 East Tropicana Avenue
702 739 8484
www.afrenchbouquet.com

FLOWER LAS VEGAS
702 451 9005
www.flowerlasvegas.com

ELEGANT CREATIONS & CELEBRATIONS
1103 East Tropicana Avenue
702 739 9440
www.elegantcreationsforyou.com

CHILD CARE
ABSOLUTE BEST CARE
2920 North Green Valley Pkwy.,
Suite 321
Henderson, NV
702 990 0944
www.absolutebestcare.com

PHARMACIES/ DRUG STORES
SAV-ON DRUGS: 24-HOUR PHARMACY
9100 West Sahara Avenue
702 254 6065
www.savon.com

SHOPPING
BELLAGIO
3600 Las Vegas Blvd. South
702.693.7111
www.bellagio.com/pages/shops_via.asp

DESERT PASSAGE
Inside the Aladdin Hotel & Casino
3663 Las Vegas Blvd. South
888 800 8284
www.desertpassage.com

FASHION SHOW
3200 Las Vegas Blvd. South
Las Vegas, NV 89109
702 369 8382

FORUM SHOPS
Caesars Palace Hotel & Casino
3500 Las Vegas Blvd. South
702 893 4800
www.caesarspalace.com

GRAND CANAL SHOPPES
Venetian Hotel & Casino
3377 Las Vegas Blvd. South
702 414 4500
www.venetian.com

LE BOULEVARD AT PARIS
3645 Las Vegas Blvd. South
Las Vegas, NV 89109
702 739 4111

WYNN ESPLANADE
Wynn Las Vegas
3131 Las Vegas Blvd. South
702 770 7100
www.wynnlasvegas.com

Gamblers in the pool at the Sands hotel, ca. 1954.

COPYRIGHTS

Pages 4-5: © Lindsay Hebberd/Corbis; page 6: © Michael Keller/CORBIS; pages 8-9: © Susan Gallagher/Michael Abramson; page 10: © Thinkstock/Alamy; pages 12-13: ©Ambroise Tézenas; page 15: ©Assouline Publishing, Inc.; pages 16-17: © Photofest; page 19: © Bettmann/CORBIS; pages 20-21: © Assouline Publishing Inc.; page 23: ©UNLV Library Special Collections; pages 24-25: Andrew Zuckerman/Big Magazine; page 26 top: © Lake County Museum/ CORBIS; page 26 middle: © UNLV; page 26 bottom: © Bettmann/CORBIS; page 27 top: ©UNLV; page 27 bottom: © Lake County Museum/CORBIS; pages 28-29: © Bettmann/CORBIS; page 30: © Bettman/CORBIS; page 32 top: © Bettmann/CORBIS; page 32 bottom left: © Picture Net/CORBIS; page 33 top: UNLV Library Special Collections; page 33 bottom right: © Bettmann/CORBIS; pages 34-35: © Assouline Publishing Inc.; pages 36-37: © Michael Abramson and Susan Fowler-Gallagher; page 39: © Magnum Photos; pages 40-41: © Assouline Publishing Inc.; page 42: © Photofest; page 43 top left: Bettmann/CORBIS; page 43 top right: © Photofest; page 43 bottom: © Photofest; pages 44-45: © Photofest; page 47: Pictorial Press/Alamy; pages 48-49: © Bettmann/CORBIS; page 51: © Photofest; page 52-53: © Burt Glinn/Magnum Photos; pages 54-55: © Photofest; page 56: © UNLV Library, Special Collections; page 57 top left: UNLV Library, Special Collections ©; page 57 top right: © Photofest; page 57 bottom: © UNLV Library, Special Collections; page 58: © Roxanne Lowit; pages 60-61: © UNLV Library, Special Collections; pages 62-63: © UNLV Library, Special Collections; page 65: © Assouline Publishing Inc.; pages 66-67: © Assouline Publishing, Inc.; page 68 top left: © Assouline Publishing Inc.; page 68 top right: © Assouline Publishing Inc.; page 68-69 © Assouline Publishing Inc.; page 71: © Assouline Publishing Inc.; page 72 top left: © Haruyoshi Yamaguchi/Corbis; page 72 top right: Assouline Publishing Inc.; page 72 middle: © Photofest; page 72 bottom left: © Photofest; page 72 bottom right: © Photofest; page 73 top: © Bettmann/CORBIS; page 73 bottom: © Photofest; page 74: © Photofest; page 76: © Mitch Diamond/Alamy; page 77: © Hank de Lespinasse/Alamy; page 79: © Roxanne Lowit; page 80 top left: © Bettmann/CORBIS; page 80 top right: © Brian Lawrence/Image State/Alamy; pages 80-81: © Anders Ryman/Alamy; page 80 bottom left: © Private Collection; page 80 bottom right: © Image State/Alamy; page 81 top left: © Anders Ryman/Alamy; page 81 top right: © Roxanne Lowit; page 81 bottom right: © Private Collection; page 83: © Private Collection; page 84: © José Fuste Raga/Zefa/CORBIS; pages 86-87: © Photofest; page 88: © Assouline Publishing Inc.; page 90: © Bettmann/CORBIS; page 91 top: © Assouline Publishing Inc.; page 91 bottom left: © Photofest; page 91 bottom right: © Assouline Publishing Inc.; pages 92-93: © Assouline Publishing Inc.; page 95: © Getty Images; page 96-97: © Assouline Publishing Inc.; page 98-99: © 5Dimensional Systems by Screampoint LLC; page 101: © Bettmann/CORBIS; pages 102-103: © Getty Images Hulton Archive/Stringer; page 104 top left: © Mark Peterson/CORBIS; page 104 top right: © Bettmann/CORBIS; page 104 bottom left: © Bettmann/CORBIS; page 104 bottom right: © Bettmann/CORBIS; page 105 top left: © Popperfoto/Alamy; page 105 top right: © Bettmann/CORBIS; page 105 bottom: © KPA Honorar & Belege/Content Mine International/Alamy; page 106: © Brad Harris; pages 108-109: © Cardinale Stephane/CORBIS SYGMA; page 111: © UNLV Library Special Collections; pages 112-113: John Springer Collection/CORBIS; pages 114-115: © Corbis; page 116: © Robert Miller for Wynn Las Vegas; pages 118-119: © MGM Grand; page 120 top: © Assouline Publishing Inc.; page 120 bottom: © Assouline Publishing Inc.; page 121 top: © Burt Glinn/Magnum Photos; pages 120-121: © MGM Grand; page 121 bottom: © UNLV Libraries, Special Collections; pages 122-123: © Harry Gruyaert/Magnum Photos; page 125: © Jennifer Worthington; pages 126: © Robert Miller for Wynn Las Vegas; page 127 top: © Assouline Publishing Inc.; page 127 Middle left: Assouline Publishing Inc. page 127 middle right: MGM ; bottom right: © Franz Marc Frei/CORBIS; page 128: © Bettmann/CORBIS; page 130: © All rights reserved; page 131 top left: © Bettmann/CORBIS; top right: Assouline Publishing Inc.; bottom left: © Bettmann/CORBIS; page 132: © Richard Melloul/CORBIS SYGMA; page 134-135: Robert Essel/CORBIS; page 137: © CORBIS SYGMA; page 138 left: © Chris Farina/CORBIS; page 138 middle: © Chris Farina/CORBIS; page 138 right: © Assouline Publishing Inc.; page 138 bottom: © Assouline Publishing Inc.; page 139: © Assouline Publishing Inc.; pages 140-141: © CORBIS; page 142: © 5Dimensional Systems by Screampoint LLC.; page 144: © Jennifer Worthington; page 148: © Jeannine Henebry for Wynn Las Vegas; page 151: MGM Mirage; page 152: © David Pollack/CORBIS; Page 155 © UNLV Library, Special Collections; page 156: © Assouline Publishing Inc.; pages 158-159 © Pam Krug.

Publisher's note: Every possible effort has been made to identify legal claimants; any errors and omissions brought to the publishers attention will be corrected in subsequent editions.

ACKNOWLEDGMENTS

Thank you to Martine and Prosper Assouline for entrusting me to bring their vision of Las Vegas to life and to Esther for never getting angry when I have missed deadlines. Kate—Thank you, thank you, thank you. To my brother Paul who is my Jerry Maguire, to my parents and sister who love me enough to have moved to Las Vegas, to my beautiful daughter who makes me laugh with wonderment everyday. To my Chris who has taught me that creativity is everything and changed the way I live my life. To Kristieanne for always being there and to Elana for being my partner in crime. Thanks to Meri-Michelle for her hours in the library and to UNLV Special Collections for their fabulous archives. Most of all, I give many thanks to the fabulous characters of the past, present, and future of Las Vegas who make living in this city a truly memorable experience.